it's NOT *that* complicated

it's NOT that complicated

The Twelve Rules for Raising Happy, Self-Reliant Children

doug peine

Health Communications, Inc.
Deerfield Beach, Florida

www.hci-online.com

Library of Congress Cataloging-in-Publication Data
is available from the Library of Congress

©2002 Doug Peine
ISBN 0-7573-0004-9

Publisher: Health Communications, Inc.
          3201 S.W. 15th Street
          Deerfield Beach, FL 33442-8190

Cover and inside book design by Lawna Patterson Oldfield
Cover photo ©International Stock

To Christine,
for her love and for her patience

CONTENTS

PREFACE

I had sacrificed most of the afternoon in a futile attempt to help an estranged couple resolve their disputes so that they could avoid the cost, financial and emotional, of a divorce trial. But they were adamant. They were not going to let go of their rage, no matter how destructive it was to them, to their children, to their finances.

Later that day, as I waited in a long line at Kmart to pay for my toothpaste and double-A batteries, a headache climbing up the back of my neck, I watched the toddler in a cart ahead of me defy her hapless mother and absolutely refuse to put back the Milky Way bar she had appropriated from a box by the checkout. In that child's body language, tone of voice and insistence upon irrationality, I saw the very same conduct played out in my conference room earlier that afternoon.

We are cowed these days into believing that the behavior of our children is a subject so esoteric as to be beyond our poor powers as laypeople to fully understand.

That may very well be. But the fact remains, the vast majority of successful parents in our society are not child psychologists; they are those who, rich or poor, sophisticated or naive, are able to commit nothing more than their love and their fundamental common sense to the task of raising their children.

This work goes in search of that common sense by examining, in particular, those parent/child struggles we've all been held hostage to . . . in the checkout line at Kmart.

ACKNOWLEDGMENTS

Thanks to Nick for being such a great teacher.

Thanks to Christine Belleris and Allison Janse at HCI for being such great editors.

And thanks to Thomas Sutton, Demetre Nicoloff and Hovald Helseth.

A NOTE ON GENDER

Any writer today faces the problem of language conventions that have yet to catch up to modern sensibilities. How especially are we to use pronouns in a manner that is not gender specific?

Various solutions have been put forward. All are awkward. My ears are offended particularly by the displacement of the singular by the plural, e.g., "they" for "he" and "she."

My least disfavored option is to retain the gender specific pronouns but to attempt to use them in equal proportions throughout the course of the book. Therefore, when I talk of "her" you will understand that I also mean "him," and when I use "his" I also mean "hers," etc.

Why Would You Want to Read *This* Book?

Compromising facts, I advise my clients, are best admitted right up front. That way, maybe the jury will have forgotten them by the time the trial is over.

In that spirit let me confess that I have never taken a class in child psychology. Truth be told, I seem to have successfully dodged psychology courses of all kinds during my years in high school, college, graduate school and law school.

Why then should you even consider spending your hard-earned money on this slim volume, especially when the shelves in front of you are sagging under the weight of obviously more detailed works written by professionals who actually practice in the field?

Suffer me six more brief paragraphs to persuade you.

First, it is my observation that child psychologists and psychiatrists have proven no more successful at raising happy and well-adjusted kids than the rest of us. Indeed, if my freshman roommate at college was at all typical, there is compelling evidence a number of them have botched the job worse than we could ever have done.

This does not mean that theirs is not a worthwhile field of study. Child psychology has done a remarkable job of providing us insights into the mental and emotional development of children, particularly those who are troubled. I do not for a moment mean to disparage it.

But I do think it is obvious that those insights have not resulted in better-adjusted kids, theirs or ours.

Are today's children happier than previous, less-enlightened generations? Better fed, yes. Distracted by vastly more entertainment options, certainly. Enjoying better physical health, no question. But happier? Kinder? More resilient?

Apparently a specialized knowledge of the intricacies of the child's brain is not a blueprint for successful child rearing.

As further evidence of this fact, I observe that uneducated and unsophisticated people *who take the job seriously* have just as good a track record of raising happy, well-adjusted children as do others. Or stated in its corollary, the educated and affluent—those who have greater access to the vast contemporary literature on child rearing—do not on the whole enjoy greater success.

Too Much Information Is No Information

What this says to me is that *it's not that complicated.* Parenting is not quantum mechanics. It demands dedication, absolutely, but it does *not* require synthesis or analysis of a profusion of detail in order to be effective.

Indeed, I would maintain that many new parents who seek help from child-rearing literature, instead of being aided and comforted, are confused by an overabundance of detail—much of it contradictory.

If you're like me, you can absorb only a limited amount of information and can remember even less. The net effect of laboring through an endlessly detailed self-help manual is frustration rather than illumination. We become frozen rather than inspired.

And even with those few exceptional books worthy of careful reading, we're lucky if, a month later, we're able to recall more than a dozen significant points.

When I myself went looking for advice on parenting, I became convinced that many books on the subject are padded just to fill out a required standard length—whether or not that length is necessary to communicate the author's ideas. There may be some nuggets of wisdom in there some place, but they are near impossible to locate among the irrelevancies and redundancies.

The simple fact is, as a new parent you've never had less

time in your life to spend prospecting for those nuggets. You want crisp, confident information now—please cut the crap.

In light of these realities, this book takes a different tack. It is built upon two basic beliefs:

1. There is at work among those who parent well a fundamental common sense.
2. This common sense can be briefly stated and readily grasped by anyone.

Kmart as Classroom

Although I have never taken a psychology course, I have other qualifications you should know about.

- I am a child of parents.
- I am also a parent of a child.

That means that while I may not have studied the theory of war at the academy, I have served in the armies on both sides. And I have paid close attention.

I have paid attention especially on those trips to Kmart we must all routinely hazard for the sundry essentials of modern life. While waiting in the checkout line I have not, like you, wasted my time furtively scanning the grotesque stories in the tabloids.

No, I have found it vastly more interesting to watch the

actual grotesque stories of the parent-child struggles that are played out in that venue as in no other place on Earth. It is those stories—the dreadful, little family dramas we've all been forced to witness—from which we will largely draw the lessons in this book.

Endless Repetition

What I have observed in Kmart (and elsewhere, for that matter) are the same obvious parenting mistakes made over and over again, with the same obvious results occurring as predictably as the sun rising in the morning.

On the other side of the coin, I have been curious to observe those of my friends who have reached late middle age and who have negotiated their lives with relative ease, success and happiness. I have inquired about their parents and their upbringings, seeking to identify what it was that equipped them to handle their lives so well. What I have found are the same few features repeated over and over.

Finally, I have also been a practicing lawyer for twenty years, a profession which, if nothing else, offers a singular vantage point from which to observe the front lines of human conflict. It never ceases to amaze me how the same behaviors I see in my adult clients and their legal adversaries reflect the same structures as those parent-child struggles played out at Kmart.

And so it seems to me that I have no choice but to conclude that *it's not that complicated.*

I'm reminded of my brother's response when I asked him what his old classmates were like when he attended his twenty-fifth high school reunion: "Just like what they were in high school, except more so."

We *are,* to some degree at least, what our parents made us. And we will continue to be so until we drop. And our children will, to some degree, be what we make them. It doesn't require Freud to help us see the broad outlines of this or to advise us how we should proceed. Common sense will do. And for most of us that is the best we can hope for.

Twelve Rules and Twelve Rules Only

And so we proceed with twelve simple, easily understood rules, each followed by a brief illustration and explanation of why it is important.

Why twelve? Because more than that is too many to call to mind when needed. It's an arbitrary number, then? Certainly it is. But our goal here is not to acquire all knowledge, but just enough to work with and not feel overwhelmed by.

I recall advice offered to young pitchers by Jack Morris at the end of his long and distinguished career in baseball. To hell with complicated strategy, he said. Concentrate on just two simple principles:

1. Throw first-ball strikes.
2. Don't be afraid to pitch inside.

And he was absolutely right. Every successful pitcher abides by these two rules. There are other aspects to pitching success, certainly: velocity, mechanics, pitch selection, etc. But Morris's point was that too often a player allows himself to sink in the quagmire of minutia.

The same thing happens in child rearing. Too many parents these days have worried the details and lost sight of the basic truths. This book seeks to rediscover those truths.

Do the twelve rules described in this book exhaust all knowledge pertinent to raising a well-adjusted child? Of course not. But I do firmly believe that if these particular twelve are followed intelligently and conscientiously, you have a pretty damn good chance of ending up a pretty damn good parent.

What Exactly Is It That We Want?

I appreciate the fact that you have stayed with me this far. But now I must turn the tables and impose rules upon you if you want to continue further.

Before we discuss means we must consider ends. What kind of kid is it we want to raise? I'm going to give you my answer to that question. You are free to agree with me or not, just as you are free to buy this book or not.

Certainly each parent has his or her own individual aspirations for their child. The variations are as endless as the personalities involved, and that is all for the good. Yet, it seems to me that at the core there are essentially three common attributes all thoughtful parents want for their children—and again, *it's not that complicated:*

1. All parents want their children to be *happy.*
2. All parents want their children to be *disciplined.*
3. All parents want their children to be *compassionate* toward others.

Each of these attributes deserves explanation.

Happiness

What *is* happiness? Thousands of years of theological treatises, philosophical tomes, literary works, clinical studies and country music songs have not succeeded in answering that question with satisfaction. Certainly it is a relative term that can mean different things to different people.

Here, as everywhere else throughout this book, we take the commonsense approach. Happiness here is defined simply as the *ability to take as much pleasure in life as possible.*

Life is difficult, sometimes very painful. The fact of mortality—our own as well as that of the people we love—is largely responsible for this. But even in moments of health, life buffets us with nagging worries, lost loves, dashed hopes, ruined expectations.

At the same time, however, existence offers many pleasures. There are moments when life is nothing short of glorious, when our hearts sing, when we are delighted to be alive.

What I want for my own child is to equip him so that over the course of his life:

1. He has the tools to minimize as much as possible the painful moments.
2. He has the tools to maximize as much as possible the pleasurable moments.

This is what I believe will serve my son best, not only while he is a child in my house, but also when he is an adult on his own.

If you, on the other hand, believe that the only way to prepare your child for life is to develop him into a pit bull, then please just put this book down now. Go study Bobby Knight's coaching techniques instead. You and I have a fundamental disagreement about the nature and significance of human life.

The only reasonable goal in life, for ourselves as well as for our children, is happiness—as much as possible over the long haul.

Discipline

At first glance it might seem an awkward segue to go from happiness to discipline. The two concepts seem at opposite ends of the spectrum. But the truth is, the former is impossible without the latter.

By "discipline" I don't mean something I *do* to my child. Discipline does not mean administering a spanking or sending my child to his room when he is naughty. Neither does it mean turning my child into an automaton that does whatever I ask without questioning.

In this book "discipline" is not a verb at all. It is a noun, and one which describes a fundamental fact of the happy life: Sometimes a person must deny herself short-term happiness for long-term happiness:

- You can't eat all the candy you want now, because later it will make you sick.
- If you want to enjoy playing the violin well, then you must put up with the drudgery of practice now.
- If you want to have fun at your friend's birthday party tomorrow, then you must go to bed now and get your rest.

Exercising self-discipline is nothing more than squeezing as much happiness as possible out of life over the long term. For that reason alone it is one of the greatest gifts a parent can give to a child.

Compassion

Because we are social animals, much of our happiness is bound up in our relationships with other people. Those relationships that are successful bring us much pleasure. Those that are unsuccessful cause us great pain.

I suggest to you that those relationships—whether intimate or casual—that bring the greatest fulfillment are those in which we recognize and respond to the humanity of the other person in some fashion. By that I mean simply this:

1. We do not forget that others suffer the same mix of pain and pleasure as we, and
2. For that reason we act in the manner best calculated to contribute to their pleasure and ease their pain.

And so if we are six years old and have a candy bar, we share it with a friend.

Or if we are forty years old and our attorney wife is depressed because she lost a big case, we make every effort to remind her of all the cases she has won and help her regain her perspective.

Or if an acquaintance loses a loved one, we take the time to send a note of condolence because we recognize that the gesture will help ease, in some little way, her sense of loss.

Or if we are entering a doorway and notice the person

behind us laden with packages, we stop and hold the door for him.

Or if someone needs to enter our lane of traffic to make an exit, we slow down to let her move in front of us.

Or if a panhandler approaches, we worry less about being duped by some con artist and more about refusing someone who needs help.

What these examples describe in its basic form is selflessness, or perhaps more accurately, a lack of selfishness. Or perhaps even more accurately, a lack of solipsism.

Solipsism is the notion that because I can only know my own consciousness, mine must be the only one. All the rest of you are simply actors in my world. It is a philosophical concept, but it is also a convenient psychological device that allows us to feel no remorse for running roughshod over other people's feelings in pursuit of our own agenda: They must not suffer the way I do because when they are hurting *I* don't feel a thing.

Of course it's an absurd notion when spelled out. But that doesn't mean we don't exploit it on those occasions we feel the need to dupe our conscience into letting us get away with a selfish act or two.

Kids especially are able to avoid the fact that their self-centered actions often hurt others. Those kids who never learn otherwise grow up to be miserable human beings.

We're not talking in moralistic terms here. The question

we need to ask ourselves throughout this book is simply: "What can I, as a parent, teach my child so that he has the best tools for experiencing as much happiness and as little pain as possible over a long life?"

Self-discipline is one of these tools. Compassion and kindness are others.

Parents Must Also Recognize Their Limitations

The debate between nurture and nature continues largely unresolved. Which behavior is learned? Which is the unavoidable result of one's chemical makeup? What parts of our children's mental and physical development do we have control over and what parts do we not? Let me add further to my credentials by admitting that I don't have a clue as to how to answer these questions with any precision.

Certainly, a parent does not have *unlimited* control over the development of a child's personality. This is especially evident among kids with conspicuous physical and mental disorders.

We cannot deny the fact that no book on child-rearing techniques, no matter how detailed, can provide all the answers to all parents, or indeed all the answers to any one parent. It only makes sense, then, that a very significant part of parenthood is recognizing and accepting the fact that there are limitations to influencing a child's life.

On the other hand, there is a dangerous modern tendency at all levels of society to refuse to accept responsibility not only for our children's actions but our own. "That's just the way I am," people are heard to say, especially when it provides them a convenient excuse for not doing something they don't want to do.

Or we attribute our child's ill manners not to our failures as a parent, but to his attention deficit disorder or her depression. It's as though we are incapable of exercising any control whatsoever over our children's lives, and so the world is just going to have to put up with their undesirable personality traits.

There is no question that prior generations punished certain conditions and behaviors that we now recognize are the results of brain anatomy, not personal choice. There is no question, as well, that happiness is to some degree the result of the genetic and chemical mix coursing through our veins. And certainly we must be sensitive to these fixed aspects of our own and our children's personalities.

But at the same time, we have no alternative but to continue to assume that a significant part of what a child becomes is largely influenced by the choices we, as parents, make in raising her.

It is to these choices that this book attempts to speak.

Parenting Is Hard Work

If, in fact, *it's not that complicated* to raise a happy, well-adjusted child, then why do so many do such a poor job of it? Apart from issues of confused thinking, which this books attempts in small measure to clear up, the answer, I believe, is that while *it's not that complicated,* it isn't necessarily that easy.

While the major principles of successful child rearing are finite in number and readily understood, putting those principles into practice is where most people fail. Why is this? Because to parent well requires time and effort.

Time

Parenting cannot be accomplished in absentia. You must be there in person, and you must be there a lot. If you are not yet prepared to sacrifice your own personal agenda, whether it be career-related or recreational, then you shouldn't have a child. If you have a child and still refuse to make the sacrifice, then you are acting irresponsibly as a parent. (We will not mince words in this book.)

Of course, many parents are simply in a bind. They have to work long hours in order to support their children. They have no choice. But there are many more parents who *do* have a choice—and make a bad one.

For example, say you work long hours and are able to

spend only a little time with your child during the week. Then every Saturday you take off with your pals to play golf for four or five hours. Guess what? You're being a selfish jerk and should be ashamed of yourself. Of course you need your recreation and diversions. But your child needs you more. *It's not that complicated.*

When you have a child, your life has to change. And not just a little. Radically. If you want to be a responsible parent, sacrifices of time have to be made. Too many men and women have children and then expect to carry on with their old lives as though nothing has changed. Our kids are paying the price.

Effort

Successful parenting oftentimes means having to select the most difficult among the options presented to you. This is what I mean by "effort."

For example, your child is learning to tie her shoes and wants you to witness her progress. You have a tough work day ahead and are anxious to get going. The easier choice is to convince yourself there's no time for it now and just tie her shoes for her. The harder choice is to recognize that this is important to her and that one more minute is not going to make any difference to either of your schedules.

Or say your five-year-old wants one more piece of candy

from his Halloween stash before going to bed. You know he's already had too much, that he's simply acting out his reluctance to let go of a day in which he's had so much fun. To complicate matters, maybe you said something to him earlier you shouldn't have, and you're feeling guilty about it. The easier thing to do is to just let him have the candy. It will make him happy in the moment, and that will, in turn, make your moment easier.

Or say it's late in the evening and your ten-year-old hasn't yet practiced her piano lesson. You know she is tired and will balk when you remind her. You're tired, too, and the last thing you want is a struggle. And so the easier option is just to let her go to bed.

The right choice in each of these situations is obvious. That's not the problem. We know what we *should* do. The problem is doing it. Unfortunately, there is no shortcut here. The simple fact is, parenting requires some of the hardest work, bar none, you will ever perform during the course of your life.

But the effort required is easier to summon if, rather than getting lost in the confusion of contradictory information, you pursue a strategy in which you have confidence that you are doing the right thing and will achieve the desired results.

Effort is also easier as it becomes habitual. If you start using the principles in this book when your child is very young, and if you are consistent in applying them, sooner or later they will become second nature to you and your child.

Truth is, the act of parenting can make you a better person—better disciplined, more understanding, more patient and certainly more loving.

The intent of this little book is to give you the confidence to foster those habits in your child *and* in yourself in light of the fact that *it's not that complicated.*

Mean What You Say

"No, No." A Thousand Times "No"

It just couldn't be simpler: When you say "no"—which you have to do often when raising a child—you must mean it. The way you show that you mean it is by enforcing it. Immediately. Not tomorrow or when you get home. Now. No hemming and hawing, no stalling or waffling, dallying or dawdling. Right now. This instant. There simply is no other way for a child to learn what is acceptable behavior and what is not.

When your three-year-old grabs a box of cereal off the shelf at the supermarket, tell her "no" and ask her to put it back. If she refuses, take it from her, put it back yourself, and inform her that when you get home she will have to suffer an appropriate punishment for disobeying you.

If she decides then and there to throw a tantrum, tell her to stop it. If she refuses, remove her from the area, take her home, and impose a more severe punishment.

A child's bad behavior is like a goldfish; it will take up as much room as you allow it. But if you apply consistency, gentleness and firmness, you will not have problems. *It's not that complicated.*

How Dare You Permit Your Child to Show You Disrespect

If you do not consistently follow this simple rule, you will lose your child's respect. There are few things uglier. You will lose your child's respect because she will come to realize that Dad will not follow through on his threats, or that Mom won't enforce her authority—in short, that her parents *don't* mean what they say.

Mom says, "Stop that." The four-year-old blithely disobeys, confident through experience that Mom won't enforce her words.

Mom says, "Stop it, or else." The child continues her bad behavior, knowing the threat is an empty one.

Mom says, "I said 'Stop it.' And I mean it." The child, glint in eye, grin on lips, does "it" again with relish.

Mom gets specific. "Stop it, or I'll take your toys away from you." Still the child keeps on, assured by history that even this threat is hollow.

What a frustrating scenario to watch, especially since it is so easily avoided.

You Are Making You *and* Your Child Miserable

The irony is that the child enjoys this dance no more than the parent. It is a disturbing thing to discover that your parents cannot be depended upon; that, in fact, they are liars.

Next time you observe a child being insolent toward his parents, look closely and you'll likely spot anger pulsing among the other emotions of the moment. It's an anger that arises out of the fact that the child has been denied his fundamental sense of security. *If Mom doesn't mean what she says when it comes to controlling me,* he thinks, *then how can I trust anything else she says? If she doesn't have the guts to enforce my behavior, how can I trust her to have the guts to protect me?*

Your child is relying on you to show him how to negotiate the perilous mountain road of life. He needs to have confidence in your ability to not take him careening off the edge.

If he observes that you can't control a little kid like him, how can he expect you to have any capabilities with the really tough guys out there in the scary world? Who's going to protect him and show him the way? Certainly not you. You've betrayed yourself as unfit. Apparently he's going to have to make it on his own.

What a blow to a kid. No wonder he's angry.

And no wonder that each time he's offered the opportunity to stick it to you, he'll seize it. Each time he has a chance to defy you, he'll do it in the way best calculated to cause you the greatest humiliation. Because if you're not going to provide him the security he needs, he's going to at least eke out a measure of consolation in the simple pleasure of taking his anger out on you.

That's what this behavior has become for him: recreation. After a while, it has little to do with whatever is the subject of the moment: toys, refusal to go to bed, punching his sister. It is now nothing more than the simple pleasure of getting in your face and proving once again what a moral coward you are.

Soon enough he'll be initiating trouble just to get the fun started.

Painful to Watch

Ahead of me in the checkout line at Kmart is a father reading a tabloid while his three-year-old girl squirms in the shopping cart. Her heels kick the cart, her lips hum a song, her eyes roam round and round for some escape from boredom. She notices a display rack within arms' reach.

"Daddy," she says.

"What?"

"I want gum."

"No gum." He doesn't raise his eyes from his reading.

She is irked by the inattention. She kicks out a foot that

rattles his paper. This brings a bright smile to her face. He jerks his paper out of reach, refusing still to make eye contact with her.

"Daddy," she says again.

"What?" There is irritation in his voice now. Yet she shows not the slightest hint of being intimidated.

"When are we *going!* I want to *go!*"

"Pretty soon," he says, still insistent upon being preoccupied.

"But I want to go *now!*"

"Sorry. Gotta wait in line." He flips over a page. She looks at him hard and calculatingly. She happens to catch my eye and holds the gaze. Her forehead furrows and her mouth presses out a pout. *How dare he treat me like this?* her expression says.

She turns in her seat and begins plucking packs of gum from a display box and tossing them into the shopping cart. After about the fifth one Dad has no choice finally but to look up.

"Stop it," he says.

"We need gum," she says matter-of-factly, tossing more packs into the shopping cart.

"I said 'Stop it.'" He closes up his paper in an effort to show he is serious. Too late.

She wrinkles up her nose and actually sticks her tongue out at him. Then she steals a glance at me expecting, I suppose, to bask in my admiration of her audacity. But I'm too busy wincing.

Mercifully he does *not* slap her. But neither does he do anything constructive.

"Stop it," he says again, his impotence now as obvious as his five-o'clock shadow.

She raises her nose another inch in the air and tosses a couple more packs of gum into the cart.

Father and daughter stare each other into a standoff until it comes time for Dad to roll forward to the cashier. He does so, taking his daughter out of reach of the gum. He begins to gather the items in his cart and set them on the conveyor. She watches him closely and bides her time.

When everything else has been placed on the counter, he collects the packs of gum from the cart and begins fitting them back in the display boxes. She's been waiting for this.

"Gum!" she hollers. "I want GUM!"

"No," he says quietly.

"GUM, GUM, GUM, GUM, GUM . . ."

Her chant grows louder and louder until in desperation he takes the last pack, cups it in his hand, furtively drops it in among his other purchases on the counter, then steps back as though the gum had fallen from the sky. She quiets immediately and gives circumstances a little nod of approval.

A few minutes later, after I have paid for my purchases and pause to slip wallet into pocket, I notice father and daughter just outside the plate glass window, heading for the parking lot. They have stopped on the sidewalk. The father is unwrapping something. I look to see what it is. He hands his daughter a stick of gum, and she folds it into her mouth. She notices me through the window and gives me a big smile.

It's Your Own Damn Fault

Obviously gum was not the issue. It was an enjoyable little perk, certainly, but what this little girl was mostly about was reaffirming her moral authority over her father. She made him squirm, and it was a fun way to pass a few otherwise boring moments.

Let us acknowledge the obvious: There is absolutely no excuse for allowing matters to deteriorate to such a point that we become ashamed of ourselves as parents. Especially when all we have to do is say "no" and mean it.

It's not that complicated.

Never Strike Your Child

The Most Asinine of Proverbs

And the winner is: "Spare the rod and spoil the child."

What rubbish. It's one of those unenlightened and illogical clichés incurious people fall back on instead of assuming the responsibility of thinking for themselves. The needless pain and psychological damage that have been inflicted by dumb adherence to it are tragic.

We don't permit corporal punishment of even our worst criminals. Why should we do it to our children? The simple fact is this: there is nothing positive that spanking can achieve that noncorporal disciplinary measures cannot.

And so, bottom line, unless you want to teach your child that it is appropriate for the stronger to physically hurt the weaker, there is no legitimate reason to ever hit your child. *It's not that complicated.*

The Menacing Emotion

Nineteen times out of twenty, physical punishment is inflicted not as the result of the parent's calm and rational assessment that it is needed. It is done for no other reason than the parent is angry and wants to vent. Thus the line between corporal punishment and abuse is very, very thin.

In the heat of the moment, which is when most physical punishment occurs, a spanking is nothing more than a parent wanting to haul off and hit something. At heart, then, it is a selfish act by the mother or father and most definitely not a legitimate tool of parenting.

Who's in Control?

But, say some, a parent has to show the child who's boss. Bull. It's obvious who's boss. You're older, bigger. You have control over all aspects of your child's life. You tell her when to get up, when to go to school, when to go to sleep. She is at your mercy for the food and clothing she receives.

Of course you're the boss. Maybe *you,* in your own insecure mind, need reinforcement of the fact by belting her every so often, but she sure doesn't.

The Brutality of Confused Thinking

Before you decide to spank next time, just stop and think. Exactly what is it you're trying to accomplish?

Some say it is to teach the difference between right and wrong. But that makes no sense. If a child does not know the difference between right and wrong, what right have you to punish him? Punishment is not teaching; it is reinforcement. You punish only when he *knows* the difference between right and wrong—and chooses to do wrong. At that point punishment is, at its very best, nothing more than an artificial disciplinary system intended to serve until your child develops his own self-discipline.

Teaching must always come before punishment, and so the correct order of events is this:

Step 1. Make sure that you communicate to your child that his action is unacceptable. The word "no" and a stern voice are the indispensable tools by which you accomplish this. The goal is very simple: to let him know what it is you want him to do or stop doing.

Step 2. Once that communication is accomplished and your child chooses to defy you, *then* punishment is in order.

Appropriate Methods

The key to effective punishment is denial of privileges. That's the way it works in real life.

- If we don't eat the right foods, we get sick and can't enjoy the fun foods.
- If we procrastinate and don't do our work when we're supposed to, we won't be able to play tennis later.
- If we're unkind to our friends, they will no longer want to be in our company.
- If we don't pay our bills, we lose the privilege of managing our own finances.
- If we cannot keep ourselves from acting in a way that endangers others, we lose our freedom.

If we are to prepare our children for this system, then we must impose a similar code of conduct within our homes. The trick is to link the offense and the punishment in a way that mirrors the realities your child will face in the adult world.

And thus:

- If your child won't eat her broccoli, she can't have cake.
- If she doesn't do her homework, she can't watch television.
- If she's unkind to her friends, she cannot play with them for a period of time.

- If she spends money when she shouldn't, she loses the privilege of making her own spending decisions.
- If she cannot keep herself from acting in a way that endangers others, she is grounded.

Reason, Not Brute Strength, Governs

We don't need to delve into the intricacies of child psychology to recognize the fact that spanking sends the wrong message. It says to a child that at least some forms of hitting are okay; that in some circumstances it's just fine that a stronger person exercises his dominion over another by inflicting pain.

This is not a lesson we want to teach our children, for the simple reason that our laws and our society support the opposite belief: Reason and justice rule, not brute strength.

It doesn't take any genius to see that hitting your child also perpetuates the practice and passes it down through the generations. It is the abused—from habit or misdirected retaliation—who are likely to abuse their own children.

It's tragic and ghastly, but *it's not that complicated.*

It's your duty to break the chain.

Hitting Also Hurts the Hitter

In the housewares section of Kmart, I am next to a young mother with a one-year-old boy in the child seat of her shopping cart. She and I are pooling our knowledge in an attempt to figure out how to operate a food processor displayed for sale on a middle shelf.

From his high perch the little boy reaches up to the top shelf and hauls down a Pyrex measuring cup. He obviously enjoys the grip of his little hand on the thin, smooth handle.

The mother notices what he is doing. She takes the cup from his hand and says, gently, "No, no. Mustn't touch." She replaces the cup atop the shelf and returns her attention to the food processor.

The little boy wrinkles his brow at this encroachment on his freedom. He narrows his eyes at me as if to say, *Can you believe what she just did?* He reaches up and grabs the cup.

Mom notices again, takes the cup from his hand and repeats, in the same gentle voice, "No, no. Mustn't touch." She replaces the cup on the shelf.

Now he's ticked. Before she has time to turn her attention away from him, he makes certain she sees him again take the cup off the shelf. He looks her right in the eye. It is an unequivocal challenge.

"No, no," she says again like a talking doll, "Mustn't touch." Again she takes the cup from him and puts it on the shelf. And of course he immediately grabs it back. She moves her hand to take the cup from him, and he jerks away defiantly.

"No!" he shouts at her, furrowing his brow and gritting his teeth.

Heretofore gentle Mom snaps. She grabs the cup from him and slaps his hand with a loud *smack*. For the first hundredth of a second he is stunned. After that he is shrieking. As she wheels him off toward the checkout, Mom says, loudly enough for me to hear over his screaming, "Serves you right."

No doubt she is trying to convince herself as much as me.

A Slippery Slope

There was absolutely no need for this mom to inflict physical pain had she acted thoughtfully and logically. Instead, she let the situation get out of hand; not only did her child lose his cool, but so did she.

That, I would submit, is the pattern of the majority of occasions when parents resort to corporal punishment: They lose control of their children—and of themselves.

It doesn't have to happen. In the incident just described, the first time the child grabbed the measuring cup he probably didn't know he was doing anything wrong. And maybe he still had doubt the second time. On both occasions his mom acted appropriately with her gentle voice and clear use of the word "no."

But after the third time there was no more room for

doubt. The dividing line between right and wrong had been crisply communicated to the boy. From here on out his was an act of defiance.

And so it was time to initiate appropriate punishment. In this instance, two measures should have been taken immediately:

1. Mom needed to change her tone of voice. A gentle inflection is perfect when teaching. It obviously does not work when punishing. Instead, she needed to look the child right in the eye and let him know unequivocally by her frown and her stern voice that she was unhappy with him. Her displeasure itself would have been a punishment.
2. Mom also needed to move the cart so that her child could not reach the cup. That, too, would have served as an appropriate punishment—i.e., denying him the ability to further offend.

If at this point he had thrown a tantrum, Mom's only choice would have been to calmly stand her ground and remove him from the area and the store if necessary. Sooner or later, once he understood that the status quo was not going to change, *he* would have had no choice but to relent.

That's the key: You must be steadfast until he knows his conniption will not buy him any advantage. It's not a pretty thing. But that, sometimes, is the unavoidable nature of raising a child. And you can bet that if you don't take care of business now, it will only get uglier later.

It's not that complicated.

Do Not Force
Your Child to Make
Adult Decisions

Knowledge Now, Choices Later

There is much discussion these days about offering young children a choice in behavioral matters rather than simply imposing parental will. This is all well and good, as far as it goes. But it doesn't go very far.

The simple fact is that young children do not yet understand right and wrong. Nor are they able to anticipate the consequences that result from their actions. To thrust them into a situation where they must make decisions that require knowledge of these elements is senseless. It can also end up being quite cruel.

Moral Hot Stoves

We spend a good deal of our time as parents of babies and toddlers keeping them out of physical danger. They do not understand that if you touch a hot stove you will burn yourself. Or that if you swallow an action figure you will choke. Or that if you climb out a fourth-story window you will fall to your death.

So, as the adults who *do* understand these things, we impose our will on the child. We do *not* give her a choice, for the simple reason that she does not have the capability yet to make an informed choice for herself.

This is our duty as her parent. If we act otherwise—if we simply allow her to touch the hot stove so that she learns about fire the hard way—we will be guilty of child abuse.

The same principles apply in the context of a child's behavior. Think about it. Does it make any more sense to offer her a *moral* choice when she is not yet able to appreciate the ramifications?

Who Would Ever Want to Be Selfish?

I am in the electronics department at Kmart looking for the one size of camera battery they don't have, when across the aisle from me unfolds a little drama between mother and four-year-old boy. The mother is flipping through the CD rack while her son looks about for something that might interest him. He spots it.

"Mama!" the boy says. "Lookit!"

The mother looks down to where the boy is pointing.

"Bugs Bunny!" the boy cries. He grabs a *Space Jam* DVD out of the bin. "And Michael Jordan!"

"I see," says Mom. "Isn't that nice."

The boy studies the DVD cover for a moment. Then he holds it up and says, "I want it."

"Sorry," says his mother.

"But I want it."

"Can't have it. Sorry."

"Why not? I want it."

"Because it costs fifteen dollars. And we don't have fifteen dollars."

The little boy screws up his face and ponders this for a while. He's not convinced.

When Mom finishes her business, she says, "Okay. Let's go."

She takes a couple of steps before realizing he is still standing by the DVD rack, *Space Jam* still clutched in his tight little fist. His mother looks him over. He's the first to speak.

"I want this."

Mom maintains her cool. She shakes her head and says in a calm voice, "I'm sorry, but you can't have it. So please put it back."

She makes another motion to go. Again he stays put, the DVD now clenched in both hands. She assesses the situation, considering her options. Finally she chooses. It is a bad choice.

"Do you want to put the movie back?" she asks him.

Oh, the Insanity of It All

Excuse me, but what a dumb thing to say. Of course he doesn't want to put the movie back. He just spent the last minute tightly focusing all his efforts on communicating, verbally as well as physically, that one single idea.

This is not a moment for offering a child choices. It is time for a parent to act.

You know all the reasons, financial and otherwise, why he can't have the DVD. He, in contrast, cannot as yet understand those reasons nor appreciate the ramifications.

Your only logical course of action is obvious:

1. Take the DVD from his hand.
2. Put it back in the bin.
3. Physically remove him from the vicinity and the store if necessary.
4. Impose a punishment for disobeying you.
5. Later, after everyone has calmed down, explain to him as best you can the realities of life and finances and budgets and why he could not have the DVD.

Patience to One Can Be
Injustice to Another

The strategy of offering behavioral choices to a child is especially exasperating when, as so often happens, it encroaches upon the rights of another person.

A young father and his two daughters, ages five and three, sit on a bench by the window at Kmart, waiting perhaps for Mom to bring the car around. While Dad keeps watch out the plate glass toward the parking lot, the girls play with their new, unboxed Halloween dolls. The three-year-old has a witch, the five-year-old a ghost.

Each is content with her toy until the younger girl finds a button on hers which, when pressed, sounds a funny witch's cackle. Both girls are surprised and delighted by this discovery. The younger presses the button again, and again the cackle sounds. Both girls giggle.

The five-year-old goes in search of a button on her ghost doll. Sure enough she finds one. She presses it, eyes wide open in anticipation. A brief, dull "Boo" is a big disappointment.

The two girls press their buttons a couple of times in turn. No question about it: The cackle is way cool; the "boo" is a dud. When this fact has become clear, the older girl does what tyrants of all ages have done from the beginning of history: She simply appropriates the witch as her own, handing her little sister the ghost. Of course little sister begins to cry, which hauls a reluctant Dad into the matter. But rather than meting out justice, he decides to offer the older girl a choice.

"Melissa," he says, "Don't you want to give Mary's witch back to her?"

Melissa presses the cackle button again. Mary cries all the harder.

"Melissa," Dad tries again. "You don't want to make your sister unhappy, do you?"

Oblivious, Melissa hits the cackle button. Mary is now shaking with sobs.

"Melissa, don't you think you should give Mary back her doll?" Dad asks.

Two Wrongs Make Two Wrongs

This lesson Dad is trying to teach Melissa is a double-edged sword. All Mary is learning is that her father will permit a state of injustice to continue much longer than he should. Certainly Melissa has her rights. But not when she is walking all over someone smaller and weaker than she.

This is not a time for rational discourse. Another person is suffering while Melissa gets to think about what she's done. Rational discourse comes later. Right now justice must be swift and sure. To wit:

Father to Melissa in no uncertain terms: "How dare you take something that is not yours. That is unacceptable. Give the witch back to Mary immediately!"

If Melissa hesitates, Dad should take the witch from her hand, give it to Mary, and impose an appropriate punishment on Melissa, perhaps depriving her of her ghost doll for some period of time: "Since you cannot play in an unselfish way, then you lose the privilege to play at all."

Then Dad should take the ghost doll and keep it until such time as Melissa shows proper remorse and is willing to offer a sincere apology to Mary.

Later on, after the heat of the moment has passed, is the time for Dad to explain the situation.

"Melissa, I want you to understand what happened this afternoon. You acted very selfishly in taking Mary's doll. And you made her very unhappy. You would not like it if someone did it to you. And so that is why you were punished. Do not let it happen again."

Young children do not have the capacity to make moral choices. They need to be *told* what is right and what is wrong. And they need to know that if they do wrong, then they can count on being punished. This is your job as a parent. Perform it. Don't abdicate it and force the responsibility on someone who is unqualified.

Punish Your Child, Not Your Friends

If ever you and your children are visiting at my home, let me ask you a favor. Let's say it's time for you to go, and you announce the fact to your son. He, of course, doesn't want to leave because he's having too much fun playing with my son. But it's late, you're tired, and more importantly, it's apparent to you that my wife and I are ready for you to leave.

For pity's sake, don't negotiate with your child. Please don't say to him, "Do you want to put on your coat so we can leave?" Of course he doesn't want to leave. Of course he's going to find every excuse not to do what you have asked.

Your responsibility to yourself, to me and my wife, and to your child is not to ask but to tell: "Get your coat on. It's time to go."

"But Dad," he says. "I don't want to go. We're just starting to have fun."

You say, "I understand that. But it's time to leave now. Put on your coat, please."

If he refuses again, you must act decisively: Pick him up physically, wrap him in his coat, and carry him to the car. On the way home explain the situation *and* the punishment.

"When I ask you to do something, you will do it. If not, you will suffer the consequences. I am your parent. As your parent it is my job to show you how you should act.

"Now here's the situation: Our friends were tired. They were ready for us to go. That is why we left when we did. To have stayed longer would have been a discourtesy."

It is bad enough to offer inappropriate choices to a child in any situation. It's even worse when done at the expense of your friends.

It's not that complicated.

Never Hold Grudges

Sorry, But the Good Old Days Are Over

A good deal of successful parenting involves suppressing emotions. The way you *want* to act, the direction in which your passions *want* to drag you, is oftentimes *not* consistent with your child's best interests.

Say your toddler breaks your great-great-grandmother's gravy boat. Your natural reaction is to scream and holler and burst into hysterical tears.

Sorry. You can't do any of that. It's alright to show you're upset, certainly, but you must do it in a context where you bring your rationality to bear.

Remember, your principal responsibility in life now is to dole out a reasonable and just punishment that will teach your child the appropriate lesson, which is, in this particular case, to show more care toward other people's things.

Screaming and hollering and hysteria do not get the job done. All they do is frighten and confuse your child.

This may not seem fair to you. You're hurt and you're angry. Aren't you entitled to express your emotions fully and honestly? *No,* you're *not.* That's the whole point.

Parenting is self-sacrifice: sacrifice of your time, of your money and of your emotions. You can't go out clubbing every night like you used to—your child needs you at home. You can't send off for the new fall fashions you see in the catalogs—you need to save for your child's education. You can't buy that sports car you covet—it doesn't have room in back for a child's safety seat.

And the sad fact is that you are no longer entitled to take your anger for a walk any old time it looks up at you with its leash in its mouth. That is because your child is not an adult and does not understand what that anger means.

You are trying to teach your child how not to be a jerk. You can't screw it up by acting like a jerk yourself.

It's not that complicated.

Lovely, Luscious Anger

Okay, maybe sometimes anger *does* need to be expressed. Otherwise we'll just explode into a billion pieces. The problem, though, is that it is too easily exploited for the selfish purpose of indulging ourselves in the lovely warmth of righteous indignation. And once we do indulge, we are wont to drag it out long after we have the right to, simply because it feels so good.

I have no idea what a little girl—she must have been four or five—in the checkout line at Kmart did, but her mother would not ease up on making her feel guilty.

"I'm sorry, Mommy," the girl said over and over, looking up into her mother's tight-lipped face for some softening of features and gripping tightly to the hem of Mommy's coat.

Mommy would not even make eye contact with the girl. She was steamed and was going to make the most of it. And she did, for the entire ten minutes I waited in line. As I left the store I could still hear the little girl sobbing. I don't know what the offense was, but there was no mistaking the effect her mother's anger was having on the little girl. She was desperate.

The fundamental absurdity of the situation was that Mom was treating a four-year-old as though she were an adult.

It may make sense to hold a grudge against someone who has wronged us, who has the capacity to make amends and has chosen not to do it. But a four-year-old does *not* have that capacity. She is dependent on *you* to show her the way, to teach her not only right from wrong but the protocol when she has screwed up. For you to take your anger out on her before she has been able to absorb these matters is unfair.

As her parent you have the power over the terms of her forgiveness. To hold her hostage from that forgiveness is cruel.

We must always make every effort to remind ourselves that children's brains are not sophisticated, that they perceive matters in very simple terms. As adults, when our spouse is miffed at us, for example, we are usually capable of identifying and understanding passing anger. And so, while we may feel badly for the period the friction lasts, we take comfort in knowing there is a foundation of love that has not suffered damage.

That little girl in Kmart had no such insight. She was desperate because it seemed to her that mother's love was in the balance. Quite simply she was thinking, *Mommy doesn't love me anymore.* Is there *any* reasonable lesson a child can learn from such an experience?

As we discuss in another part of this book, not only must you love your child unconditionally, you must let her *know* you love her so. You may not like the way she behaves at times, you may be momentarily angry at her when she acts selfishly or unkindly, but those lapses do *not* affect your love for her.

She will not understand this if you insist on the selfish pleasure of holding a grudge.

The Right Way

Okay. So what do you do when your child misbehaves or acts selfishly or unkindly?

1. You make her stop.
2. You impose an appropriate punishment.
3. You execute that punishment.
4. You forgive her.
5. You reassure her that while you are not happy with the way she has behaved, you love her more than ever.

Imposing a punishment and expressing love are *not* inconsistent; indeed, they must always accompany each other. If there is a key to good parenting, that is it: the balance of firm consistency and unqualified affection. The former focuses exclusively on the particular misconduct at issue. The latter is the reassurance of the unalterable nature of your love for your child, a love that endures to the grave. Even if that grave is preceded by the gallows.

Not the Key to a Happy Life

Apart from the terrible insecurities engendered when you refuse to forgive your child, there are the larger lessons of life that are taught him. To the extent that he copies your behavior, teaching him to hold a grudge is *not* fostering the habits of a contented life, for the simple reason that staying angry is by definition staying unhappy. *It's not that complicated.*

It is a fact of life that we will regularly be hurt by the insensitivity, the blunders, the misdeeds and the outright cruelties of others. Human beings are terribly flawed, and as long as we interact with them, we are bound to suffer as a result. Given this fact, how can we live so as to minimize the impact? Should we cultivate our anger so that it lasts as long as possible, so that our stomach acid churns and our blood pressure spikes?

Or should we forgive and forget, seeking justice when we can, but recognizing that injustice is a fact of life and that we are oftentimes better off over the long run accepting that fact and moving on?

Lawyers see it every day. The legal system is glutted with the grudge matches of litigants who just won't let go of their anger:

- businesspeople who would rather run their shops to financial ruin—the very same shops they spent their lives so carefully crafting—rather than forgive the perceived injustices of their former partners
- home buyers who would rather risk losing the house of their dreams for the sake of some $50 dispute with their sellers over a dilapidated gas grill
- divorce clients—especially—who sacrifice tens of thousands of dollars in attorneys' fees for no more productive purpose than to wreak revenge on the spouses who wronged them.

No question that some litigants are people of courage who rightly pursue justice at great personal expense. But way too many are people who have become obsessed with real or perceived wrongs to the point that they have lost perspective of the cost-benefit analysis. They need to ask themselves: *Is it worth it to me over the long run to sustain this anger at such a fevered pitch?*

I don't need Freud's help to imagine that little girl in Kmart twenty years from now—choosing to take the hard road through a divorce.

Take a Close Look at Yourself

There is one more reason why so many of us should not spend so much time nursing our grudges. More often than not, our anger is not entirely justified by the circumstances that have given rise to it, especially when we are dealing with our children.

It only takes a couple of years practicing law to realize that, except in rare cases, *both* sides contribute to the creation of a conflict. Only in the world of bad fiction are characters all good or all evil. In real life people are inevitably a mixture of both. The obvious lesson is, next time you're really mad about something, look in the mirror first. Are you absolutely sure you contributed nothing to the situation? Frankly, the odds are against your being blameless.

It's a difficult, subtle question, especially in the heat of the moment, but you must ask it: *What did I do to help make this mess?* It is a difficult question, yes, but looking honestly at ourselves is what we are about, isn't it? And isn't that what we want to teach our children: to make the effort, hard as it may be, to become better human beings?

I don't know the facts, but I can certainly imagine a scenario in which that mother, who was so adamant about refusing to forgive her little girl, was herself as culpable as her daughter in whatever happened between them.

With a four-year-old, especially, one must wonder if the little girl understood that what she had done was prohibited behavior. Perhaps she did commit a cardinal sin. On the other hand, maybe her mother was simply taking out her bad day on the most convenient target.

You, too, will do this. Don't kid yourself. You will take out your anger on your child when she does not deserve it. If you then allow yourself the selfish pleasure of milking that anger for as long as you can, you will only be giving yourself the opportunity to screw up all the more.

Anger can be very, very destructive, especially when an unsophisticated child is its focus. If you are going to be a good parent, then you must always be vigilant, not only for when anger first appears, but also for when it loiters.

"It's Just the Way I Am"

"But," some will say, "that's just my nature, to hold grudges."

It has become much too fashionable to abdicate personal responsibility via the claim that our fundamental character is unalterable. We are what we are, yes. But we are also what we want to make of ourselves. At the very least, we have the responsibility to do what we can to rescue our children from those of our own habits which, in candid moments, we realize have frustrated our ability to enjoy life as much as possible.

If you must insist on being so selfish and self-destructive as to hold grudges, at the very least aim them in the direction of other adults, not at your children.

It's not that complicated.

Threaten Only Those Punishments You Can Carry Out

Another Bad Decision

In the crowded housewares department at Kmart, a father makes an ineffectual effort to regain control of his wild seven- and ten-year-old boys. The boys are playing a frenzied game of tag, bouncing off the walls and displays. They obviously care little that their game is interfering with shoppers attempting to maneuver through crowded aisles.

Dad tells the boys to stop it. They ignore him entirely. He says it again. Again they ignore him. So he decides to get serious.

"I said stop it right now, or we will *not* be going to the Vikings game tomorrow. And I mean it."

This succeeds in getting the boys' attention. Momentarily. The seven-year-old studies his older brother's face. The older boy is thoughtful for a moment, then shakes his head, as if to say, "Don't worry about it." The seven-year-old laughs and chases after his brother as raucously as before.

A Hollow Threat

Apart from the other obvious problems in this parenting situation, it's clear what was wrong with the particular punishment Dad chose to threaten the boys with. They knew—at least the older boy did—that Dad would *not* carry through.

Pro-football tickets are expensive. They are not easily sacrificed, particularly on the altar of imposing punishment on one's children. Besides, Dad surely wanted to go to the game as much as, if not more than, the boys. He was not likely to deprive himself simply to teach his children a lesson. The boys knew that because: *it's not that complicated.*

Engage Your Brain

The moral is obvious: Think before you select a punishment for your child. Make sure it is one that affects him and him alone, and does not catch other innocent parties in its net. Because if it does affect others, you are going to have one hell of a time enforcing it.

And if you do carry through nevertheless, the arbitrariness of your action will teach a bad lesson about justice. Why should others be punished for something they had no hand in?

Furthermore, when you, the parent, are one of the peripheral victims, which often ends up being the case, conditions are ripe for the sort of resentment that is inconsistent with thoughtful parenting. In such situations it is all too easy to blame your loss on your child: "It's *his* fault that *I* didn't get to go to the Vikings game."

Fact is, it's not his fault at all. It was *your* dumb idea to select this from all the available punishments. He just acted badly in a way entirely unconnected to the football game. *You're* the one who dictated the disastrous cause and effect.

Punish the Wrongdoer, Not Her Sister

A parent needs to be particularly sensitive to this problem in relation to siblings. Too often the punishment of one also works as a punishment of another. That is fundamentally unfair and fosters resentment.

And so one guideline is to never mix punishments with family activities. This prohibition includes the strategy of excluding the wrongdoer from the activity. That is unsatisfactory for the simple reason that exclusion can punish other siblings to the extent that the punished one's presence is necessary to the enjoyment of the activity. At the very least it casts a pall over the event.

We're Not Dealing with Dummies Here

The image that lingered after the episode with the boys and their game of tag was the look on the older brother's face after his father made the threat. While the prospect actually caused the younger boy concern, his older brother was able to conclude with confidence from his longer history that Dad would never cancel the trip to the Vikings game.

Truth is, kids soon become experts at reading their parents in this way. That's because their very freedoms and rewards are dependent on the ability to know when Mom and Dad are in earnest and when they're not. It's a matter of survival. And so they are always walking the perimeter of family boundaries, testing the integrity of the chain link, looking for the breach that will set them free. Once they find it, they never forget its location.

And so you must try very hard to be consistent in your punishments and to always enforce them.

You must also think before you act. Don't toss off a proposed punishment in the heat of the moment. Take a few seconds at least to reason it out and run down the ramifications.

Finally, be judicious in your selection of an appropriate punishment. Make certain it not only fits the offense but can be properly executed.

Coaxing the Horse Back in the Barn

But what do you do when your mouth works before your brain engages—believe me, it *will* happen—and you actually voice a threat you know you cannot or will not be willing to carry through on?

Simply change the punishment and explain yourself: "Hold on a second. *I* don't want to miss the Vikings game. It's not fair for me to be punished for something you did. And so I change my mind. If you don't knock it off right now, no soda and no candy for a week."

As we discuss in detail in the next chapter, there is no dishonor in admitting when you are wrong.

Admit When
You Are Wrong

A Shortage of Perfect Parents

You are going to screw up a whole lot as a parent. And badly. You will holler at your child when she has done nothing worse than have the misfortune to wander into the room at the very moment you have become aggravated by something entirely unrelated to her. You will blame your child for accidents she couldn't avoid, simply because you're in a snit and want to find somebody to blame for something. You will unfairly accuse your child of misbehavior on evidence no more substantial than your hunch she might have done it. You will interrupt your child when she is talking and rightfully has the floor.

Many more times than you would ever want to imagine, you will hear that little voice in the back of your head saying, *I cannot believe I'm doing what I'm doing right now.* You will know you are wrong, and yet you will be unable to stop yourself.

We are flawed human beings, no exceptions. No one escapes. That doesn't mean we shouldn't make every effort to bring our rationality and self-discipline to bear and minimize the frequency and severity of our parenting mistakes. Still, there are going to be times when the best of us blunder and treat our children badly.

The question, then, is how to deal with that fact.

Apologize: You Have No Choice

There is only one way to deal with it: Admit that you are not perfect as a parent and that you made a mistake. First, admit it to yourself; then admit it to your child. And apologize to him.

"Apologize to my own kid? You gotta be joking! I'm his parent. Maybe I have to grovel in front of every other human being on the planet. But not him."

Oh yes, you do—if you want to raise a child with self-esteem, with a sense of justice and with an inclination for showing mercy toward others. *It's not that complicated.*

"But Mom, I Did!"

My luck this day has me in line behind a middle-aged mother with a shopping cart absolutely loaded with microwave dishes and contact-lens solution and shampoo and lamp shades and towels and sweat suits and picture frames and mops and brooms and more. Hanging off the front of the cart, because there is no room inside, is her six-year-old son.

Mom is bent over, head inside cart, sorting through her items, apparently in search of something in particular.

Finally she says to her little boy, "Sam, what did you do with that package of dinosaur underpants?"

Sam looks up with innocent eyes. "Nothin'."

"I saw you holding it. What did you do with it?"

Sam presses his lips together and thinks for a moment. "Put it back in the cart," he concludes.

"You most certainly did not because it isn't here now."

He thinks about it harder. One eyebrow goes up. "I did, Mom." He nods. "I did."

"You most certainly did not. You laid it down on some shelf when you were looking at the toys, didn't you? And you just left it there. Didn't you?"

Sam wonders, *Could all this be true?* He screws up his face and thinks even harder.

Mom hauls herself up out of the cart. "Guess you'll just have to go without underwear three days out of the week."

"But Mom, I put it back in the cart."

Whereupon Mom sets fists atop hips and gives her torso a little holier-than-thou tilt and enunciates very, very slowly, "Is that so? Well, then, Mister. Why don't you just show me where they are?"

Sam looks up from the shadow of this hulking figure, then squints toward the loaded cart and the dreadful task he's got himself in for.

Suddenly his eyes open brightly. His little hand reaches over the side of the cart and disappears into the pile of goods for a long moment before emerging with underpants firmly in its grasp. Sam holds the package high up in the air for Mom to see, a snarling raptor on the butt of a red-bordered brief.

"Here it is!" he says triumphantly. "See, Mom? Here it is!"

It was an exhilarating moment.

Mom stood stock still, her angularity unsagging. The only movement was the blink of her eyes. Finally she leaned down and looked Sam right in the face and said, "It's just lucky for you."

Immediately she turned her attention back to the items in her cart, signaling her edict that the episode had come to an end.

A frowning Sam watched her for another moment, in hopes she would put a more satisfying gloss on the whole affair. Finally realizing it was futile, he turned sadly away.

A Simple Apology Will Do

It was disheartening to watch a little boy made all the more bewildered about the whims of parental control, all the more uncertain about justice and its place in the world. It didn't have to be that way.

In the first place, Mom should not have accused her son on such flimsy evidence. You can bet she would have never tried to pull crap like that with an adult. The fact that she is probably a loving mother does not mean that in this instance, hers was not the act of a bully.

But let's grant her one mistake. The immediate question for us is how she should have proceeded once she realized she'd made an ass of herself.

The answer is clear. She should have simply admitted her mistake and apologized for her unjust treatment of Sam. A little humor would have helped:

"Here it is!" Sam says excitedly. "See, Mom? Here it is!" He holds the three-pack of underpants high.

A sheepish grin works its way across Mom's face. Her eyes open wide. "Oops," she says.

Sam smiles cautiously.

"Oops," she says again.

Sam laughs cautiously.

"I think Mom just boo-booed."

Sam laughs out loud, and his mother joins in.

Mom reaches down and puts an arm around Sam's shoulder. "Sorry," she says. "That was unfair of me to accuse you. I apologize."

Sam's eyes get a little bigger.

"Sam, everybody makes mistakes. Even moms. And when they do, they need to admit it and to say they're sorry. I should have believed you. I shouldn't have falsely accused you. I'm sorry."

Sam beams. "It's okay, Mom."

She leans down and gives him a kiss and a big hug, which he returns all the more lovingly.

Apology as an Act of Love

What did this Sam, the one who existed only in my dreams, learn?

First, he received affirmation that his emerging sense of justice was sound. *Yes,* he was able to think to himself, *I was right and Mom was wrong.*

Second, the episode boosted his self-esteem by demonstrating that justice also applies to a little kid like him.

Third, it provided him a vivid example of how painless it is to admit one's mistakes. It didn't hurt Mom in the least. Entirely to the contrary, she was able to use the situation to bring them even closer together. Quite simply—which is the only way Sam was capable of seeing things—the apology was an act of love. Contrast that to what actually happened between Sam and his mother, an experience that pushed them further apart in every respect.

Fourth, the apology enhanced Mom's credibility in Sam's eyes. A child is much more likely to accept a parent's dominion over him if that dominion is exercised fairly.

Finally, it gave Sam the opportunity to experience the joy of forgiving. His mother offered him the great gift of power over *her,* and as a result he learned that the benevolent exercise of that power can be a wonderful experience.

A Chance Worth Taking

Why was Sam's mother unable to apologize to him when she was so conspicuously wrong?

For many people these days, apologizing to anyone, let alone one's child, is anathema. It's obvious in traffic. How often has someone cut you off then sneered at you as though you're the one who did something wrong? How often do political figures, after being caught with their hands in the cookie jar, seek to scapegoat the media? How often do sports figures, their errors replayed in unequivocal slow motion on national television, blame the fans or referees or their teammates?

What everyone seems to be missing is the simple fact that frank acknowledgment of imperfection does not make us less but *more* appealing. That's because it allows everyone else to relax just a bit and not dread so much their turn to go down in flames.

Wouldn't you like to hear someone, sometime, just say, "I screwed up. I'm sorry"? So would your children.

Structure Your Child's Life So That He Learns to Be Responsible

As Good as It Gets

We are born into a world and a society whose rules are not of our own making. If it had been up to us, things might very well have been different. But it wasn't and they aren't.

So we have two choices: We either spend our lives bashing our heads bloody against the brick walls we're born inside of, or we learn the skills that allow us to negotiate the corridors of life and explore it from room to room.

The second choice is called being "well-adjusted." The first one is not.

Obviously, if what we seek for our children is the greatest happiness over the long haul, then we want them to opt for the second choice. And so it is our duty to help them learn the necessary skills.

Doors Are Opened by Firmly Grasping Door Knobs

The most important of those skills is responsibility. Being responsible means nothing more than responding successfully to the demands placed on us by other people and by society at large.

As always throughout this book, we are not talking in moral terms. Our concerns here are practical only. It is a practical fact that responsibility is a prerequisite to a happy life. For example:

- We must be responsible for our personal hygiene and dress, so that other people are comfortable being with us.
- We must keep our room reasonably neat and orderly, or we will be unable to find the things we need when we need them.
- We must treat our friends kindly and fairly, or they will no longer want to be our friends.
- We must learn to perform well on school exams, or we will not receive the grades we need to progress in our education. If we don't get a good education, we cannot get jobs that are fulfilling and financially rewarding.
- We must show up for work on time, or we will lose our job and the paycheck that comes with it.

- We must perform our work in the way our bosses want, or we will not advance to a better, and a better-paying, job.
- We must make our mortgage payments, or we will lose our comfortable home.
- We must abide by the laws, or we will lose our personal freedom.

It is not necessarily fun to fulfill responsibilities. But if we do not, our lives become considerably more difficult. Or stated conversely, life is significantly easier—and its rewards more readily available to us—if we learn to respond in a responsible manner to society's demands.

The Blessings of Habit

How do we teach responsibility to our children?

First, we need to remember that much of the pain of being responsible is relieved by routine. Once we are in the groove of responsibility, it becomes second nature.

For example, we pay our bills. We don't really want to. We'd rather use the money for dinner at our favorite restaurant, or for a new leather jacket, or for that diamond pendant we saw in the jeweler's window. But we're accustomed to sitting down each month and sending off those checks to the power company, the telephone company, the mortgage company, etc. And so it doesn't really hurt that much because we're used to the self-denial involved.

It logically follows that if our children are to assume these responsibilities in a way that makes that assumption as painless as possible, we should prepare them for the task. If we are successful, adulthood won't come as a jolt, but as a position for which they have been fully equipped.

The long-term strategy, then, becomes apparent: Expose the child to more and more responsibility as he grows and becomes capable of successfully fulfilling it.

Build It and They Will Go

Because childhood is by nature sheltered from most of the responsibilities imposed by society at large, a parent must construct artificial ones within the family. For example, a young child may be required to simply put her dirty clothes down the laundry chute every night. Not a big deal, and certainly not a chore that saves Mom and Dad any appreciable labor. But the artificiality of the responsibility is irrelevant. It is the commencement of a *habit* that is important. As the child gets older, her responsibilities may become more meaningful. For example:

• She may be required to set the table for dinner every night.

- She may take music lessons and be expected to practice every day.
- She may be asked to help fold laundry.

The options for responsible tasks are endless. The only condition required is that they demand something of the child that she is capable of doing.

Gradually, society will nose its way into her life and impose its own requirements on her, especially once she begins school. At that point, the parent's job is not so much to fabricate responsibilities—although, of course, the child must continue to have her chores at home—but to make sure responsibilities are consistently met.

Endless Vigilance

Habit cannot develop without consistency. Every single day, for a long time, you are going to have to remind your child to put her clothes down the laundry chute. Every day. *It's not that complicated.*

It's not complicated, but it *is* difficult. How much easier it would be one night to just pick up those clothes yourself, especially when you realize she hasn't done it herself until after you've tucked her in bed. How much easier it would be when you come home late one evening to not make her practice her violin.

But you can't give in. Habits are very fragile. When they break, they usually shatter into thousands of pieces.

Bribery in Its Proportion

If done in moderation and with intelligence, there is no reason in the world why you can't reinforce your child's developing sense of responsibility with a system of rewards. That's the way society in general works.

- We suffer through school so that we can enjoy the rewards of knowledge, as well as a good job and good income.
- We practice for hours at the driving range so that we don't embarrass ourselves on the first tee at the golf club.
- We pay our taxes so we don't have to go to jail.
- We cut down on our fat intake so that we don't die in our forties of a heart attack.

Again, the reason why we practice responsibility is to create the greatest amount of happiness over the longest period of time.

There is no reason not to mimic this system with our children, especially when those responsibilities might not have their own obvious rewards.

For example, if your three-year-old successfully puts her laundry down the chute for a week, why not reward her with a piece of candy? And explain yourself to her:

> I just want to let you know how proud I am that you've picked up your clothes every day this week without having to be told to do it. You have been very responsible. Here's a little treat from Dad and me to show you how much we appreciate it.

Such an act of gratitude emphasizes the point in her mind and helps her remember her responsibilities. And it certainly doesn't do her self-esteem any harm either.

Your Chance to Become the Person You Always Wanted to Be

Bottom line, your child's developing a sense of responsibility is dependent upon your successful fulfillment of *your* responsibility.

You're going to have to get in the habit of making sure he gets in the habit. Just as much as he wants to skip piano practice and go to bed, you want to skip having to hassle him about it and go to bed yourself.

It's not easy, especially since—let's face it—many of us never developed the same sense of self-discipline we are now trying to instill in our children. How are we going to get our children to practice the piano or pick up their clothes—consistently—when we were never able to get ourselves to do it?

There's the rub. To be good parents requires that we perform at a level we have not yet been able to achieve.

Well, the time is now. When you were childless, maybe it was okay to delay your adulthood. But no longer. Now you have the solemn responsibility and sobering task of teaching another life how to negotiate an extremely challenging world. If you approach that task with determination and with love, there is no doubt you will succeed magnificently.

Never Belittle Your Child

A Matter of Perspective

One of your responsibilities as a parent is to understand as best you can what is going on inside your child's mind and heart. And to act accordingly. You must make every effort to see life from his perspective. Only when you understand that perspective are you properly positioned to respond to him.

It's not that complicated.

Too often it is too easy to simply assume that your child is reacting to events in the same way you or another reasonable adult would react. You must give yourself pause to view matters in the context of his limited experience and knowledge. Then you must take that perspective very seriously.

The Cruelty of Thoughtlessness

A mother and her four-year-old boy wait just ahead of me in the checkout line at Kmart. Among the gauntlet of displays arranged on either side of them for impulse buying are various discounted videos, one of which, as best as I can see, is about an evil leprechaun. The video cover is green, and in the middle is the picture of a small figure wearing a derby and a malevolent grin.

The four-year-old has his face pressed against his mother's thigh, except when curiosity tempts him to take another quick peek at the video display. His mother notices what is going on. She plucks one of the videos from the display and studies it.

"You afraid of this little guy?" she asks.

He says nothing.

"You afraid of a little picture?"

Again nothing.

"How can you be afraid of a picture? A picture can't hurt you. That's just silly."

He hugs his mother's leg harder. She looks up and catches me watching. That's my mistake.

She says to me, "Have you ever seen such a ridiculous little boy? Afraid of a picture that can't do him any harm?"

The little boy peeks out to see who his mother is talking to. He gives me an indignant frown, as if it were my fault.

I am now in league with Mom, and she isn't about to let me go. She winks at me as if to say, "Watch this."

She looks down at the boy wrapped around her leg.

"Don't you want to see this picture of this little man?" She holds the video next to his temple.

Nothing from the boy.

"Don't you? Huh?" She nudges his ear with the video.

Nothing, except to cling a little harder.

She nudges him again. "Come on now. Take a look. Just a little look." She's laughing now.

"No," he finally says. He says it emphatically with a poignant mixture of anguish and indignation.

She shakes her head, still laughing, still holding me hostage. "Have you ever heard of such a thing? What a little scaredy-cat."

The Clutches of Fear

The simple fact is, little children *can* be terrified by pictures. They do not have the experience or the mental wherewithal yet to sort out fact from fancy. Nor are they able to quell fear, irrational as it may be, once it rises up.

Mom would have understood this if she'd just taken a moment to use her brain instead of her mouth. She would have realized that, within a child's frame of reference, this little boy's reaction was entirely appropriate. Her failure to see this and her insistence upon holding him to adult standards were her first mistakes.

Her next was to belittle him. Even if the standards she used to judge his actions had been fair ones, there was no excuse for treating him like that.

Giving her the benefit of the doubt, I suppose she figured she was doing him a favor. Her intent, thoughtless as it may have been, was probably no more sinister than to try to shame her son out of his fearfulness.

That was where I came in. Embarrassing the boy in front of a convenient stranger was a way she saw to displace fear. And indeed, for adults, shame can be a very potent impetus to courage, a means by which we buck up and get beyond our terrors.

But this is not a lesson we need to be taught. It comes naturally to us. We don't need any parental guidance here, thank you very much.

Besides, think of the downside. This mother certainly did not do her son's self-esteem any favors. Unable to see what we can see—i.e., that he was being unfairly judged by adult standards—he was left to believe an untruth—namely, that only "silly" kids are afraid of scary pictures. Within his frame of reference he had no choice but to feel himself less worthy.

More importantly, his mother betrayed his trust, especially when she brought me into the situation.

A child has the right to expect you, as his parent, to fulfill your obligation of teaching him how to maneuver through a very frightening and demanding world. He doesn't deserve to be humiliated whenever he slips up.

The Commitment of Loyalty

There will be times when your child embarrasses you. She will say something silly or stupid in public, something you feel does not reflect an accurate picture of you and your family and your values. Or she will fail in some way to perform up to the standards you expect.

You will be sorely tempted in these circumstances to distance yourself from your child, as the mother in Kmart did, by making a joke at her son's expense. But what a cruel thing to do. What a miserable betrayal of a parent's loyalty.

This is your child, for good or ill. She needs to be able to trust you completely. Never betray that trust. Never.

Long, Vivid Memories

I had a client, one of three sons who, together with their father, were in litigation over the breakup of the family's construction business. It was an ugly legal brawl. Grown men were not only tearing apart their business but also their family. The hatred was palpable.

My client, the oldest of the brothers, detested his father with a passion so intense it had to have had more than one cause. His mantra throughout the ordeal was, "Don't trust the old bastard." At every turn of the case, in response to every conciliatory offer that came from his father's lawyer, the son simply refused to do anything but assume the worst motives. This was one angry man.

During the course of lengthy litigation, an attorney comes to know his client intimately. You spend long, long hours together in intense circumstances, working hard, despairing together when things go badly, exulting when they go well. It is like combat—without the bullets whistling overhead.

In that context you often find yourself serving as a fox-hole father-confessor. One night over dinner my client sat back in his chair, his weary face flushed by a couple of glasses of wine, his anger for the day spent. He spoke softly and sadly about his relationship with his father.

It's not so much that I think he's out to do me intentional harm. I don't believe he especially enjoys hurting me. That's not why I don't trust him. I don't trust him because I could never count on him to make the effort to try to understand what was going on inside of me. And if he wouldn't do that, then I could never trust him to make the right choice when it came to my well-being.

He drained the dregs in his wine glass, ran fingers through his hair, then leaned forward onto his arms.

"What I could never count on," he said, looking off in the distance, "was that he would be there for me when I made mistakes."

There were many, many problems in this family, and this may not have been the most serious one. But then again, maybe it was.

Praise Your Child Again and Again

Pearls Before Swine

A mother and daughter play catch with a football they have borrowed from the shelf in the sporting goods section at Kmart.

I had noticed them earlier in another part of the store. The girl is thirteen or fourteen years old, dressed in a baggy T-shirt and jeans that do not hide the fact she is overweight. Her long, straight brown hair is stringy and unkempt. Her face is spotted with acne. She shuffles with teenage angst.

The mother appears to be in her early to mid-forties and is strikingly slimmer than her daughter. *Her* jeans are tight on a small butt and slender thighs. She holds her chin high, and she chews gum in a loud, snapping manner.

When I come upon them again in the sporting goods aisle, the dynamics have changed. The girl is now animated and having great fun with the football. She also shows considerable skill. She catches well, and nearly every one of her throws puts a nice, tight spiral on the ball.

The mother is having difficulty. She is fearful of catching the ball and throws awkwardly. It doesn't take a genius to see that the source of the girl's enjoyment is the fact that for once she is performing better than her mother. She will make a skillful throw which Mom will usually drop. Mom will gracelessly chase down the flip-flopping football, then make an awkward return throw which, but for the girl's skill, she would not be able to catch.

But the mother absolutely refuses to acknowledge this fact. Not once do I hear her say, "Nice catch" or "Nice throw." Instead, she hoards her comments for the rare instance when the girl's toss is less than perfect. "I'm supposed to catch that?" she says, fists on hips.

Mom makes one particularly bad heave, the ball misdirected at a display of tennis-ball tubes neatly stacked atop one another. If the football hits the display, the entire thing will topple in a clatter.

The girl deftly redirects her body, arms extended, and snags the ball in the tips of her fingers. She has even surprised herself. Her eyes open wide with the thrill of victory. Eyebrow raised, she looks at her mother, ready for the recognition she deserves.

Mom returns the look for a long moment. She doesn't smile. Finally, she turns away, sport over. "Lucky catch," she mutters.

Makes You So Mad You Want to Spit

What in the world did that mother think she was doing? Granted, there was a history between these two about which we can only speculate. But it doesn't really matter what sins that girl had committed in the past. There was no good reason for her mother to deny recognition of her skill.

Everything about the girl reflected low self-esteem: her weight, her unkempt hair and acned face, her slouching posture. We can't know for sure if these features can be traced to the way her mother has treated her, but Mom has to be considered the prime suspect.

Apparently, the daughter is not living up to Mother's expectations, and so, in punishment, Mother is withholding all positive feedback. What a selfish, cruel and destructive thing for a parent to do.

Another Long and Vivid Memory

Although I have never specialized in family law, I have been involved in maybe a dozen divorce cases. In at least half of those I have been present to hear my client or his or her spouse work their way through the tangles of their emotions to finally identify what they believed to be the crux of the problem. It usually goes something like this:

He never praised me. He never said I did a good job with anything—raising the kids, keeping the house, juggling my own career. He's just like my father. Neither one could ever begrudge me a compliment. And so I have spent my life feeling like crap about myself. And I'm sick and tired of it.

Obviously there are features here arising from the particular dynamics and stereotypes in the relationship between the sexes. The basic problem, however, is transcendent. Men's version, in its conventional form, goes something like this:

She never appreciated the fact that I worked my butt off every single day. I'd get a promotion and come home, excited to tell her. And instead of her saying, "Nice job," she'd ask about somebody else in the company who maybe was working his way up the ladder faster than I was. And so my pleasure in my success would be deflated—just like she stuck a pin in a balloon. She's just like my dad. Nothing was ever good enough. I'd get three hits in Pony League and he'd wonder why I grounded out to shortstop my fourth time up.

Hasn't Anybody Around Here Seen *The Bad News Bears?*

Praise your children often and fullheartedly. Focus on their accomplishments not their mistakes. They desperately need it. How much more obvious could it be? The constantly fault-finding parent has even become a stock movie villain.

Why then don't we learn? I suppose some parents who refuse to praise their children believe they are pursuing a strategy that will spur their children on to success. Keep them hungry, the theory goes, and they will continue to strive.

Maybe so. But is low self-esteem a reasonable price to pay? How many more desperately unhappy sports figures and actors and musicians and politicians and workaholic businesspeople must bear witness before we get the message?

My Child, My Rival

Some parents fail to praise their children not as a strategy but simply because they find it difficult to do so. It doesn't make sense. Why would we ever resist making our children feel good about themselves?

The answer lies somewhere in the same complex of psychological reasons that explain why many of us have difficulty praising any of our fellow human beings. Since we in this book are eschewing psychological complexity, we can for our purposes here approximate those reasons with one word: *envy.*

It is a sad fact of human nature, but it is a fact nonetheless: Sometimes the good fortunes of others are very difficult to accept. Their happiness is not necessarily our happiness, especially when our less successful circumstances are in contrast.

This can be so even when those others are our children whom we love. It is hard to admit, but sometimes we begrudge the fact that our kids get to wallow in the carefree pleasures of childhood while we have to spend our time drudging our way through the trials and tribulations of the adult world.

Then, too, the promise of their lives is still ahead of them, while we grown-ups have developed our potential pretty much as far as it's going to go. Who among us is entirely satisfied with his lot in life? Who would not like another shot at it all?

That is what our children give to us vicariously: another shot at it. Oftentimes we take great delight in their successes for that very reason. But sometimes, for the same reason, we are envious of them.

It is a feature of human nature we must admit to if we are to get past it.

Praise Indiscriminately

And we must get past it. We must praise our children again and again, no matter how hard it might be for us. We must seize every opportunity to lay it on as thickly as possible.

Who, after witnessing the light in a child's eyes when she is told how well she has done something, could argue otherwise?

- We must praise them when they draw a picture, even if to our eyes it looks like chicken scratches.
- We must praise them when they play their cello, even if it sounds like a floor sander.
- We must praise them when they catch the football, and we must also praise them when they fall flat on their face trying to kick the soccer ball.
- We must praise them when they offer a piece of their candy to their baby brother.
- We must praise them when they put away their toys.
- We must praise them when they tie their own shoes.
- We must praise them every single day as often as possible.

Soon enough they will learn the hard facts of the dog-eat-dog world. Now, while they are young, is the time for fostering the self-esteem that will later help them come to terms with those hard facts.

READER/CUSTOMER CARE SURVEY

6757058862

We care about your opinions. Please take a moment to fill out this Reader Survey card and mail it back to us.
As a special **"thank you"** we'll send you exciting news about interesting books and a valuable **Gift Certificate**

Please PRINT using ALL CAPITALS

BA1

First Name _____ MI. ☐

Last Name _____

Address _____

City _____ ST ☐ Zip _____

Phone # (_____) _____ - _____   Fax # (_____) _____ - _____

Email _____

(1) Gender:
○ Female
○ Male

(2) Age:
○ 13-19   ○ 40-49
○ 20-29   ○ 50-59
○ 30-39   ○ 60+

(3) Your children's age(s):
Please fill in all that apply.
○ 6 or Under   ○ 15-18
○ 7-10   ○ 19+
○ 11-14

(8) Marital Status:
○ Married
○ Single
○ Divorced / Widowed

(9) Was this book:
○ Purchased For Yourself?
○ Received As a Gift?

(10) How many HCI books have you bought or read?
○ 1   ○ 3
○ 2   ○ 4+

(11) Did this book meet your expectations?
○ Yes
○ No

(12) How did you find out about this book? *Please fill in ONE.*
○ Personal Recommendation
○ Store Display
○ TV/Radio Program
○ Bestseller List
○ Website
○ Advertisement/Article or Book
○ Catalog or Mailing
○ Other _____

(13) What FIVE subject areas do you enjoy reading about most? *Rank only FIVE.*
Choose 1 for your favorite, 2 for second favorite, etc.

	1 2 3 4 5
Self Development	○○○○○
Parenting	○○○○○
Spirituality/Inspiration	○○○○○
Family and Relationships	○○○○○
Health and Nutrition	○○○○○
Recovery	○○○○○
Business/Professional	○○○○○
Entertainment	○○○○○
Sports	○○○○○
Teen Issues	○○○○○
Pets	○○○○○

BA1

9396058864

(25) Are you:
○ A Parent?
○ A Grandparent

**(18) Where do you purchase most
of your books?**
Please fill in your top TWO choices only.
○ General Bookstore
○ Religious Bookstore
○ Warehouse / Price Club
○ Discount or Other Retail Store
○ Website
○ Book Club / Mail Order

**(20) What type(s) of magazines
do you SUBSCRIBE to?**
Fill in up to FIVE categories.
○ Parenting
○ Sports
○ Fashion
○ Business / Professional
○ World News / Current Events
○ General Entertainment
○ Homemaking, Cooking, Crafts
○ Women's Issues
○ Other (please specify) _____

Never Fight with Your Mate in Front of Your Child

How Stupid Can We Be?

One of the most selfish and destructive things we could ever do as parents is play out our marital disputes in the presence of our children. And yet so many of us do it. And so often. The ill effects are obvious and significant:

1. In the child's eyes the stability of the home is threatened.
2. The child is put in an absolutely impossible position of divided loyalties.
3. Usually the child absorbs a goodly amount of guilt, assuming that the conflict between her parents is somehow her fault.
4. The child learns that it is okay for those who love each other to treat each other like crap.

It's a Partnership, Not a Grudge Match

Alan, a friend I came to know when I represented him in purchasing the first of several restaurants, is one of the kindest, gentlest men I've ever met. He seems to be able to accept life on its own terms and enjoy nearly all of it.

One day over lunch in one of his bistros we were talking about our kids and the way we were raising them, and about our parents and the way they raised us. He insisted to me that he never saw his mother and father argue.

"Never?"

"Not once," he said. "I know now that of course they did disagree about things, especially on how to raise me, but they never did it in front of me.

"For example, I'd ask whether I could go to a friend's house to play. Dad and Mom would both be there, and maybe Mom would say, 'Sure.' Dad would then put his hand on Mom's shoulder and say kindly, 'Sylvia, I need to talk with you.'

"They would step into the other room, return a minute or so later, and Mom would say, 'Your father tells me you didn't weed the garden as he asked you to do. So we've talked about it and decided you have to finish that chore before you go.'

"Or sometimes maybe she'd say, 'Your father is concerned you didn't finish mowing the yard. I explained to him it was my fault because I asked you to help me clean the garage. And so we've talked about it and decided that you can go, but you must be back by four o'clock so you can finish the mowing before supper.'

"They always used those words: 'We've talked about it and decided. . . .'

"I remember being at friends' houses and seeing their parents grouse and snap at each other. I couldn't believe it. For me it was an essential comfort to know not only that my parents had respect for one another, but that their respect for me kept them from arguing in my presence."

The lesson here is as powerful as it is obvious: Don't argue in front of your children. Period.

It's not that complicated.

Take It Outside, Pal

When your spouse does something in the presence of your child that rouses your anger, keep it to yourself until you and your spouse are alone. Of course it's difficult, but the task is crystal clear. Mark it down as just one more of the many ways in which parenting demands self-sacrifice.

Damage Control

Admittedly, few of us are as perfect as Alan's parents. So what do we do when our attempts at repression fail, when some spousal discord spills out in the presence of our kids?

Our obligations in that case are obvious.

1. We must talk to our children and explain the situation.
2. We must reassure them.
3. We must apologize to them.
4. We must apologize to each other.

For example:

Mom and I want you to know that we're sorry you had to hear us arguing. That was not right to put you in that position. We will try our best not to do it again. But we also want you to understand that Mom and I love each other and always will, and the fact that we may sometimes get angry with each other does not affect that love. Just like with you. Sometimes we are upset at things you do. But we always love you. The same is true between your mother and me.

And I also want to apologize to your mother. I was wrong to say the things I did.

Most minor incidents don't require anything nearly so elaborate as the above. Something along these lines will do nicely: "I want to apologize to you and Dad for me snapping at Dad a few minutes ago. That was unfair to him. And it was unfair to you. I apologize to both of you."

It's difficult to understand why this is so hard for so many people. The sense of relief, warmth and connection that follow in the wake of an apology are some of the finest moments of life, bringing those we love closer to us than ever before.

Be Prepared

All public disagreements between spouses are ugly. Those that involve decisions about the children are the ugliest. The comfort my friend Alan felt was the solidarity his parents showed when making decisions that affected him.

> I knew they were working *together* to raise me, that it was a joint effort. I could hear them discussing things at night, after I'd gone to bed. It was a real partnership in raising me, pooling their knowledge and their perspectives and trying to work out a plan between them on what to do in certain situations. They took it very seriously. It was a lesson for me in how people can work together to accomplish things. Now as a grown-up I can appreciate the way they sacrificed their own

agendas for my benefit. I can't tell you how much I love them for it. I only hope I'm doing half as well with my own kids.

Apparently, in light of Alan's spectacular success in the very difficult and risky enterprise of being a restaurateur, some of that lesson also spilled over into his business sense.

The World's a Stage

Parenting is sometimes like theater. You coordinate your actions and your responses in the way best calculated to bring out the finest in your child. To do this well, you and your spouse must rehearse certain scenarios. For example:

- What will we do if she asks about sex?
- What is our fallback plan if he gets tired and grouchy at the wedding?
- How best can we get her to eat her vegetables?

You must anticipate and talk about these things with each other off-stage. Three words are key here: communication, communication, communication.

You must also review your past efforts together in an attempt to discern what works and what doesn't. And remember always to be self-critical.

When it comes to any difficult task, two heads are a decided advantage over one. If you're lucky enough to have that advantage, for God's sake use it.

Apples and Oranges

It's appalling how many parents permit themselves to compete for their child's affections. What a lousy thing to do.

A mother's relationship with a son or daughter is *different* than a father's relationship. Not better or worse. Just *different*.

At certain times of the day or during certain activities, the child will be closer to his mother; at other times he will be closer to his father. During some stages of a child's life he may prefer to be with one parent or the other, until another stage kicks in and the dynamics change.

Sometimes it is the parent herself who, because of career or emotional needs or physical demands, must direct substantial attention away from parenting for a while. At such times the other parent is there to take up the slack, until the needs change again.

These are the natural ebbs and flows of life and relationships, and they should not be the source of jealousy. No one—not a lover, not a parent—is an appealing person when jealous.

You must simply accept the fact that sometimes your child will want your spouse more than you. As long as you are giving your child your time and your love, you can rest assured you will be securely established in his life.

Good Cop, Bad Cop

You must always be on the watch for any attempt by your child to play one parent off the other. The classic case, of course, is a child getting a "no" from Mom and then, on the sly, asking the same question of Dad. To wit:

Child in the living room: "Mom, can I have a Coke?"

Mom: "No, you may not. You had one at lunch."

A minute later child in the kitchen: "Dad, can I have a Coke?"

Dad: "Sure, why not."

Another minute later, child with Coke in hand blithely strolls into the living room.

Mom: "I thought I told you no Coke."

Child: "Dad said it was okay."

Whereupon Mom is irate at Dad.

Every kid tries this, and every kid enjoys some success. Your only hope against such a formidable force is solidarity. You must make it clear to your child that when one parent says something, it goes for the other, even if the other would have handled things differently. When one is committed, the other is committed. For good or ill.

It's not that complicated.

The Devastation of Divorce

Finally, I can't leave this subject without weighing in briefly on the subject of divorce.

It has become a cliché to say that kids are better off when their habitually fighting parents finally separate. Like most clichés I suppose this one has a grain of truth in it. But it is also constructed of a couple of dubious assumptions.

One is the unspoken premise that habitually fighting parents have no control over their conduct. It's as though spousal combat is inevitable. Certainly there are those couples whose relationships have deteriorated to such states of disrepair that divorce is the less undesirable alternative. But one must wonder whether there are many other couples who exploit the cliché as an excuse for selfishness.

Divorce is absolutely devastating to kids. There is no getting around the fact, as much as we may have tried to convince ourselves otherwise over the past several decades.

And *because* divorce is devastating to kids, you have a profound obligation to do everything you can to not let it happen.

Despite what we see in the movies and on television, no marriage is wall-to-wall bliss. There are periods in every long-term relationship when husband and wife dislike each other, when they are attracted physically to other people, when they feel their lives have been stifled by their spouses.

But you made a commitment to your spouse. And more importantly, you made a commitment when you had children not simply to create a family but to thrive in it.

In light of that, you better have a pretty damn good reason to think about divorce.

Read to Your Child
Every Night

At first glance, some might think that reading to a child, while a pleasant indulgence, doesn't quite qualify as an essential feature of successful child rearing.

They would be dead wrong.

It is one of the most important things a parent can do for a child. For a number of reasons.

Time Together

Most fundamentally, reading aloud to a child at bedtime means spending time with her in a comforting ritual when she needs it the most.

And it is not just spending time with her. It is doing so in the most meaningful of ways: blending imaginations, telling stories, sharing ideas, developing language. If you must insist on using the dreadful phrase "quality time," this is an example of it.

It's a dreadful phrase, by the way, because it provides a ready excuse for parents to act selfishly: "I don't have to spend *lots* of time with my kid so long as the time I do spend is 'quality time.'"

But who's to say what is and what is not "quality time"? Sitting in the same room with your child reading a newspaper while she watches cartoons may be quality time insofar as all she needs in the moment is to know you are there.

No, as much as we may want to believe otherwise, quality time simply is no substitute for quantity.

Easing a Child's and an Adult's Fears

Reading to a child at any time is good. Bedtime is the best.

Night is frightening for children (and for adults, too). It is the period of darkness, of ego disintegration, when our insecurities sprout horns and claws, when we cannot deny our aloneness. It is the time when we confront sleep, life's trial run of death.

To give a child ideas and stories from books with which to displace those fears is to perform a wonderful kindness. And it is a kindness that works for a lifetime. What an invaluable gift to know, no matter how trying your day has been and how difficult your tomorrow will be, that there is always a book to crawl into before sleep.

I had a client who suffered through an extremely painful divorce. Her husband, among his other atrocities, kidnapped their children and hid them in a motel for a week. I have never seen a person so anguished as she was during that ordeal.

When it was all over, the children safely returned and her husband properly dispatched from her life, we had a celebratory lunch. I asked her how she made it through those tough nights when the kids were gone. She gave me a one-word answer: "Books."

Every night, no matter how tired she is, she reads before shutting out her light. Sometimes if she is especially sleepy, she makes it through only a sentence or two. But the simple act of taking book in hands provides her the absolutely dependable sense of escape and security she needs before she closes her eyes.

Television does not get the job done. Apart from issues of content, the pictures come ready-made with TV, and so the mind's eye, the place we occupy before we go to sleep, is not engaged. We no longer see the pictures from the television screen after we've closed our eyes, but the images our imagination has sketched from words continue to develop color and detail until our consciousness folds itself up into sleep.

The Importance of Words

Obviously, reading to a young child is also crucial for developing language proficiency. The ability to use language well is a skill, and the earlier and the more often a child is exposed to it, the more skilled he will become.

Stories and books bring to our children words at their best, introducing into the home not only new ideas but also new vocabulary and syntax—and the splendid possibilities of language.

Such exposure is critical because the ability to use words well is key to a happy life, for a couple of reasons.

Life Is Just So Much Easier

Most fundamentally, of course, language skills are necessary to negotiate our day-to-day lives. Success in our education, our career, our recreations, our obligations as citizens and our relationships with our friends, all largely depend on our ability to express what is on our mind or in our heart in any particular moment.

It follows, then, that those who can read and write well have an easier and richer time of it than those who cannot.

Furthermore, language is not simply the medium for expressing ideas. It is also the raw material out of which ideas arise. To grasp complex thoughts without the ability to express them is near impossible. And anyway, what real value do thoughts have if they cannot be expressed to others?

Emotional Release

In addition to the practical rewards that come with the ability to use language are the emotional ones. How often do children, as well as adults, lash out physically because they are unable to express themselves verbally? Violence too often is the fallback position for words. Here's a typical story:

A half-dozen Cub Scouts in their blue shirts and yellow neckerchiefs rampage in Kmart while their beleaguered pack leader waits impatiently to pay for a Coleman stove.

Enjoying the safety of numbers, the boys poke each other, jump on each other's backs and chase each other. The pack leader spends his time scowling at the leisurely pace of the checkout clerk and wondering why he didn't leave the boys in the van.

I notice one boy, conspicuously the smallest of the group, off to the side by himself working on some slender object in his hands. He stops another boy and takes him aside. I can't hear what is said, but I see the first boy offer the second boy gum from a pack of Juicy Fruit.

The offeree pulls a stick from the pack only to have a spring trap snap down over his finger.

"Ouch," he yells, jerking his hand back and sticking his finger in his mouth. He frowns while the little kid laughs.

"It's not funny, man. It really hurts."

The little kid laughs harder.

The second kid puts his fists on his hips and waits for the first kid's laughter to subside. Which it does. The second kid looks his friend right in the eye.

"You really think that's a way to treat a pal? You really think hurting somebody else is fun? Then you're a jerk." He turns away, his anger vented, and goes back to join the others.

The first kid frowns. This was not the response he'd been counting on. He loads up the pack to try again.

He gets the attention of another kid—this one a big, hulking boy, almost twice the smaller boy's size. The smaller boy holds out the Juicy Fruit. Thick fingers pull at a stick. The trap is sprung with a snap.

"Yeow!" says the big kid. He looks at his finger, assessing the damage, then at his laughing nemesis.

"You, you, you . . . ," he stammers. His hands gesticulate as though looking to grab words from the air. He clenches his teeth, shakes his head, and finally just slugs the little kid in the arm.

The Lesson Is Apparent

I have in my legal career represented three men who admitted to physically abusing their wives or girlfriends. The reasons why these men did what they did are psychologically and socially complex. There is not one controlling feature to explain their behaviors.

However, among the various factors involved, each of the men at one point during my inquiries—or those of therapists appointed in the cases—said essentially the same thing: "I hit her because I didn't know how else to let her know how I felt."

Certainly there are many people who are able to express themselves verbally and still cannot contain their proclivity toward physical violence. But that does not mean that there are not many others who are able to vent through words, to *say* how they feel, and thus have no need to resort to physical violence.

Words *can* make the difference. For that reason alone you have a solemn duty to help your children to learn to use them well.

Let Your Child Know You Love Her Unconditionally

The Indispensable Ingredient

It is clear to me that the most crucial feature of those of my adult friends and acquaintances and clients who are able to take life with the greatest equanimity is their absolute certainty that their parents loved them.

Such confidence seems to provide a rock-solid foundation that is essential if we are to be able to accept our sorrows and to enjoy our pleasures.

Love Without Pretext

We must first identify the nature of this love.

It is elegantly simple.

It is not love that is earned, but love that simply is. No strings attached.

This little girl is *your* creation. You chose to give her life. That means you have the obligation to love her no matter what. *It's not that complicated.*

And that means that even if she commits mass murder and eats the corpses raw, you will be in that courtroom providing her all the support you can. For the simple reason that you have no choice. Because she is your daughter. And because you are her mother.

True parental love is *not* love of a child's accomplishments. It is not the reward for finishing homework or for scoring the winning basket or for playing the piano perfectly at recital.

Such love that is offered conditionally may be the way to drive your child to success in a particular endeavor, but it is not the way to nurture a happy life.

Certainly there are many driven and successful adults who are happy. But if you look more closely you will find they are usually the ones who were given the freedom to choose their vocations themselves, not had those vocations thrust upon them by their parents.

They are the ones who, with a twinkle in their eye, talk about how they fell in love with a basketball the first time they held one in their hands, or how dazzled they were upon seeing their first ballet.

They are the ones who were not forced down certain roads selected by their parents but were exposed to the entire map of human endeavors and given the freedom to follow the route *they* wanted, even if it was not in a direction their parents understood or appreciated.

Love for Sale

Our concern is not just with those who have been forced by their parents to play football or enter beauty contests. Coercion can be subtle as well as conspicuous. All it requires is for a parent to somehow convey to a child the sense that if I do what Mom wants, *then* she will love me.

Is your child pursuing her gymnastics or his hockey because that is truly what they want to do? Or is it because you have conveyed to them, directly or indirectly, that is what *you* want them to do, and if they do it and do it well, *then* you'll shower them with the love they need?

The Role of a Lifetime

Your job is not to select a path for your child and drive her down it. It is to expose her to the vast range of human endeavors and recreations.

In sports, for example, introduce her not just to your favorite, say football, but the others as well: basketball, baseball, soccer, hockey, tennis, swimming, running, volleyball, skateboarding, etc. Somewhere in there she'll find the one or two she really enjoys. And who knows, maybe it'll happen to be the same as yours.

Introduce her not just to classical music, but also country. And reggae and blues and jazz.

Not just the violin, but also the electric guitar and the trombone.

Not just television but film and theater and dance and stand-up comics.

Not just hamburgers but also smoked salmon and pesto.

Not just zoos and museums but also amusement arcades and county fairs.

Not just poetry readings but also demolition derbies.

Not just professional wrestling but also public radio.

You are your child's guide to the vast spectrum of life. What a thrilling role for you to play.

Always There

Dan, a dentist and a business client of mine, now in his late forties, plays guitar in a local blues band a couple of nights a week. I am familiar with Dan's financial profile and so can say with confidence that the money the band earns is a pittance compared to what Dan rakes in capping teeth.

Dan plays music simply because he enjoys it.

"The first time I heard Muddy Waters," he says, "I fell in love with the blues. And I've loved it ever since. The hours of pleasure and release I've enjoyed playing that music, I can't tell you."

When Dan was five years old, his mother started him on violin lessons. It was not his choice. His mother, a cellist in a chamber orchestra, wanted her son to have a classical music background.

When Dan discovered the blues at age twelve, he asked if he could switch from violin to electric guitar.

> She laughed at me at first. But I pestered her until she couldn't deny that I was serious about it. So she thought about it for a while, then made a deal with me. I could learn to play guitar on condition I also stayed with the violin at least until I graduated high school. I agreed. Funny thing is, I know now I wouldn't be nearly as good a guitarist had I not continued with the violin. Playing guitar is a breeze in comparison.

Dan fulfilled his end of the bargain. And so did his mother. At age eighteen he set aside his violin lessons and devoted all his musical energies to blues and to rock and roll.

> I was in a band from the time I was fifteen until my middle twenties. In those ten or so years, my mother, who hated rock and roll with an absolute passion, missed only a hand-ful of my gigs, and then only because she was sick or had other commitments she couldn't shake. Otherwise, she was *always* there, never conspicuous, but always there. I'd think to look for her in those dark dance halls and gyms and

taverns, and there she'd be, standing back in some dark corner or sitting at some table, sometimes with a friend, most times by herself. I'd get home late, and if she was still up she'd tell me how good I sounded on a particular tune. Or she'd leave me a note.

I don't think she ever acquired a taste for the music. I think she hated it to the end. But there she unfailingly was.

Here's the punch line. Dan's current blues band plays different nights during the week, but never on Tuesdays. That's the night he plays viola in a string quartet with his mother.

It's Your Child's Life, Not Yours

Your motives for pressuring your teenager into playing high-school football, as you did when you were his age, may seem benign. *All I want,* you may think to yourself, *is for him to have the opportunity to enjoy the same things I did.*

And if your son is so inclined, you may be right.

But is he really so inclined? That's the question. Does he know he has a choice?

This is a subtle, difficult issue. It demands that you be scrupulously honest with yourself. Does your son really know that it is his decision whether he plays football or flute in the band? Does he really know that you will love him equally whichever he chooses?

He is a different person than you. And thus his job is not to give you one more vicarious opportunity to relive those high-school years you're so nostalgic for.

Keep It to Yourself

When your daughter strikes out with the tying run on third base, you have every right to share in her disappointment. But you most certainly do *not* have the right to let her see that disappointment.

You're her parent. She is crushed. Your job is to do whatever you can to make her feel better, not worse. Go to her, hug her, tell her you love her more than you ever have in your life. *It's not that complicated.*

Love Without a Hitch

Love must never be the instrument of discipline. A child must never feel that if he does bad, he will risk losing a parent's love. As we've seen, there are other more effective and certainly less destructive ways to inspire your child to do well.

Let us also remember that the issue is not what you think your child *should* feel but what he *actually does* feel. You can't simply assume the message got through. This is a child we're talking about, not a logician.

Thus it is absolutely essential that you take specific actions to make sure your child understands the nature of your unconditional love.

When she is bad, you must show her that you are unhappy with her in the moment. But you must at the same time assure her that you never stop loving her.

All you have to do is say it. Wait until after emotions have calmed, then:

"I want you to know that I am very unhappy about what you did. It is unacceptable behavior, and I will not tolerate it. And so that is why you have been punished. But never forget, while I am sometimes unhappy with you, sometimes angry at you, I never stop loving you."

Sternness and expressions of love are not mutually exclusive. Indeed, the two linked is the only way to help children understand a difficult concept: The reason you are punishing them is because you love them.

Love That Is Crystal Clear

How should you show your love to your child? In whatever way is necessary to get the job done.

And what is the job? It is *not* to relieve your guilt. Nor is it to communicate love in a way that you *think* will be understood by your child.

Your job is to communicate your love to your child in

whatever way is necessary for her to understand the fact unequivocally.

If you think about it, there are really only two ways to accomplish that: (1) words and (2) physical affection.

But for many of us, such verbal and physical expressions of love are difficult to muster. Why is it so easy for some to say "I love you" while others simply can't choke out the words?

Surely it has at its root something to do with our varied responses to the fact of mortality. All persons who love each other will someday be separated. Some cope with this dismal fact by loving intensely. Others find it necessary to keep a certain distance. We all deal with life and death in our own ways.

And yet, one must be skeptical of those who say they can communicate their love to their children by means other than the verbal and the physical.

Maybe when those children grow up and gain adult insight they will appreciate their parents' sacrifice and come to an understanding of their parents' commitment to them. More than once have we heard some celebrity reflecting back on her childhood, saying something to the effect that now, as a grown-up, she knows that Dad, although he never actually said it, really loved her; otherwise he would never have provided so well for her.

But such reflections are always tinged with sadness, with regret that this revelation has come so late. Unstated is the recognition that she would have been saved a lot of grief had she understood that love earlier in her life.

And so, as hard as we try to cut slack for those who have difficulty verbally and physically expressing love to their children, we simply can't avoid believing that both are indispensable to a well-adjusted child.

You must tell your children you love them. And you must do it in these very words: "Don't ever forget, I love you now and always will."

And you must say it consistently and often. Your child must know that over the long haul, no matter what the bumps and jolts of the particular moment, your love for him is the one dependable thing he can count on.

If you have difficulty doing this, you must work at it.

And you must *show* love by touch. We all learn early enough that words can lie. Taking the risk of holding another body close to yours is the one unequivocal way of expressing love.

At heart we are all lonely souls trapped inside the vessels of our bodies. Physical affection is often the only balm.

Children, especially, are in need of touching, if for no other reason than they are foreclosed from more subtle, sophisticated expressions of love. You must hug them, hold their hands, kiss them. And you must do it often and consistently.

What our children need is the confidence that the foundation will always be there, that no matter what happens,

Mom will still be back there somewhere in the shadows of that seedy bar watching us, supporting us.

Those of us who don't have that foundation spend the rest of existence looking for it in one usually self-destructive way or another. The rest of us can get on with our lives.

It's not that complicated.

ABOUT THE AUTHOR

Doug Peine was born and raised in Lexington, Illinois, a small farming town located a hundred and fifty miles south of Chicago on historic Route 66. He received a bachelor's degree from Elmhurst College, a master's degree in English literature from the University of Wisconsin and his law degree from the University of Minnesota. Since 1978 he has practiced law in St. Paul and Minneapolis, specializing in criminal and civil appeals. He has published several articles in legal publications. This is his first book. He is married to Christine Scotillo, also a lawyer. They have one son, Nicholas, and reside in St. Paul.